Nonprofit Organization
How We Established Ours

by
Anne Louise Grimm

authorHOUSE®

AuthorHouse™
1663 Liberty Drive, Suite 200
Bloomington, IN 47403
www.authorhouse.com
Phone: 1-800-839-8640

First published by AuthorHouse 1/14/2008

ISBN: 978-1-4343-4551-6 (sc)

Library of Congress Control Number: 2007907938

Printed in the United States of America
Bloomington, Indiana

This book is printed on acid-free paper.

Dedicated to
Survivors of abuse

WOMAN . . . JUST DO AS YOUR
HUSBAND TELLS YOU!

[*Reverend Pumphandle: He has only one message,* "We must dig deeper." Men of the cloth—and until fairly recently most all of them were men—often follow the traditional line that women have no right to complain no matter how they are treated.]

Books by Anne Louise Grimm

Memoirs

Intimate Reflections
Two Years at the Panama Canal

Intimate Reflections
Tales Told out of School

Fiction
Terralimbo
Out of Time

Something Fishy
At the Panama Canal

Fletter Cove
Romance and Relationships

How-to
Nonprofit Organization
How We Established Ours

HOW DID I KNOW YOU DIDN'T ALWAYS JUST FALL DOWNSTAIRS?

[_Doctor Zitz:_ is sure it wasn't his fault that he graduated at the foot of the class. The abused—whether mothers protecting their families, or children and the elderly coerced into silence—will long hide their problems and even bruises from medical staff.]

[Basically, the first 12-page pamphlet (of an original seven) with copyright 1989, was a sample bylaws meeting State of Washington requirements—designed to be changed to fit whichever organization could use it.

Selected for revision because it sold well, the third printing was only slightly revised, with a 1997 copyright.]

> As a "dutiful wife" and which pleased him, I had listed the name of my retired husband after we had relocated—repatriated—as the author both times. Letting him take credit for being a part of Tiptoe Literary Service, my small publishing business.

[Pamphlets in a number of categories eventually totaled well over three dozen among other offerings. The most important of them were revised and reissued.]

[The pamphlets in the "Keys to Success" series were only part of what I was publishing and manufacturing in house.]

At the end of the long abusive marriage—forty-seven years of lying and hiding from family, friends and the general public that the marriage had been a mistake, learned not many months after vows taken—I used past experience in helping set up nonprofit organizations—and a copy of the bylaws to adapt—to post on my website. The response was nationwide and worldwide, asking for help. So, once again single, I self-published a little book, copyright 2001.

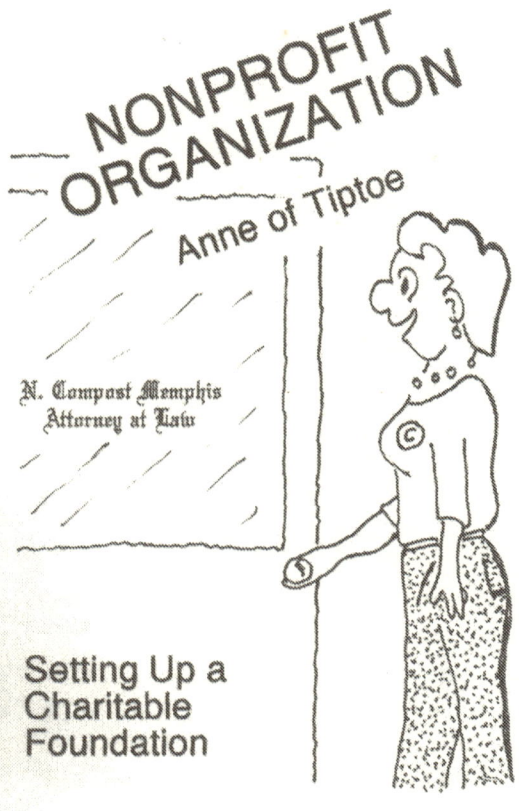

[The Nonprofit Organization title—due to its popularity—went from pamphlet to small coil-bound book.]

Putting my life together after the divorce, and disbelieved by those who had believed my earlier lies about the condition of the whole marriage, I self-published the book on the subject of abuse, removing most of the explicit directions from my website. Each year since, copies of that little book have sold, more in 2007 across the country, than in the beginning. With no more copies on hand, instead of printing more I decided to take it out of print and expand in a rewrite.

It was a good time, as I had published in 2006, four other manuscripts as books by AuthorHouse, which I could not have handled through my *Tiptoe Literary Service* business.

NOT EXACTLY A WILL . . . MORE OF A **WON'T**

[Cartoon characters led by outspoken Oyvie Oyster, lent themselves all too easily to the subject at hand.]

The complete revision and expansion from 64 pages is a short history of how a small group of us with either personal experience or knowledge of what others have gone through, slowly went about starting the nonprofit, ***Willapa Chapter DAWN, Domestic Abuse Women's Net***.

- An Episcopalian lay preacher had been one of those helping me through rescue by the Crisis Support Network and sat beside me as advocate in court every step of the way through the divorce—no, not my lawyer—she had done me more harm than good . . . and I have the letter in my files proving that. This minister, married, studying toward ordination, signed the papers for the state along with me, to establish Willapa DAWN.
- The pastor of the local Wesleyan Church—a never-married woman—when I needed help on being brought to a subsidized housing apartment from the domestic violence shelter, loaned me a makeshift mattress, folding table and chair . . . since I had none of my own belongings.
- These two women agreed to, along with me, be the first three directors of DAWN. A number more associated with the local subordinate Grange—women and men both, the males agreeing to be non-member and non-dues paying advisors—we accepted.

Stamina!

WHEN THE MEN
ALWAYS DANCE IN
SMALLER DIAMETER
CIRCLES? ? ?

[*Oyvie* recognized the unequal treatment, but usually managed to cope on her own.]

- A family needing to get away does not have the resources—wealth—that moves mountains known as judges and attorneys.
- Work by the Grange in Southwest Washington counties of Pacific and Wahkiakum had earlier established Eleanor Roosevelt Day as the Second Monday in August. Backed by State and National Grange in 1994 by passage of Resolution 94-62.
- Laws had been passed over the years, beginning well before my 1985 repatriation, at state and national level, making escape and rebuilding of damaged lives easier. It was still not easy—but easier—to get away.

- Dangers loomed and I found Washington State "Community Property" law meant only a <u>possibility</u> to fight for your rights. The court system wasn't—isn't—on the side of the afflicted, but of the powerful.

DISCLAIMER

We are not responsible for misuse made of information set forth herewith.

The author has no legal credentials, and any adaptations made of material presented, needs for safety's sake, be under the oversight of an attorney.

<u>The information is presented simply to provide help, not necessarily in setting up yet another such an organization, but for suggestions on procuring scarce direct assistance, monetary and otherwise.</u>

<u>*Locally, money for us was unavailable—though there were people willing to set up a chapter.*</u>

[*Hisa Pinhead*: Another of those men who has such a fine opinion of himself, he doesn't realize his most attractive attribute is wealth.]

We went ahead with only a slight hope of succeeding . . . As could have been done anywhere with the outline, had any who inquired wanted to. But no, most simply wanted more of what was freely given, not paying for the book in which it appeared.

One of the problems was the usual refusal to take women seriously . . . "put-downs" abounded.

INTRODUCTION

Because of the prevalence of domestic violence and the difficulties in getting out of such situations despite laws which have increasingly made things much easier, I documented my own problems as example for others as to what to avoid.

This—while a general guide to setting up a nonprofit organization—began as outline establishing a way to overcome the then prevailing domestic violence climate. It originally included:

What is a Nonprofit Foundation
Sample Bylaws Outline
Foundation Funding

The manuscript was published in rough form on the website.

Sales have been slow, but steady, year after recent year. And only for the latest edition have we added background on how our nonprofit organization itself was established.

> ## Willapa Chapter DAWN
> ### Domestic Abuse Women's Net

- We give the reason the organization was started—when and why.
- Linking to a day honoring Eleanor Roosevelt has become an integral part of this organization.

Setting Up DAWN:

A net for <u>Internet Networking</u> and a <u>Safety Net</u> spread across the United States—other countries welcome to adapt as their laws may make possible—to protect children everywhere. Intended as a way to get action more independent of lawmakers and courts, so the most helpless can afford it.

Helping reform and bend the legal system to support others wearing the same shoes we do. Women who, like us, always carefully looking out the window from behind curtains, looking over their shoulders whenever walking fearfully along a sidewalk.

Too many young mothers around our country and world are destitute, even unable to hire a lawyer, while their abusers have control of the entire income and can hire any corrupt attorney to influence judges. Judges and attorneys are too often unfeeling, macho womanizers.

Insure Justice

Hit the oppressors where it hurts most, in the pocket book. Make it more worthwhile for any attorneys already as much a help as they can afford; spur improvement of those who are a problem.

The traditional monetary reward can be offered by establishing local foundations nationwide, and eventually worldwide, to collect money for hiring selected attorneys.

Always the best available, while more learn to improve, even if just for their own enrichment.

Join the accumulating e-mail list of interested parties who want to learn how to set up such foundations in their areas, by letting them know you want to be on a Bcc: list.

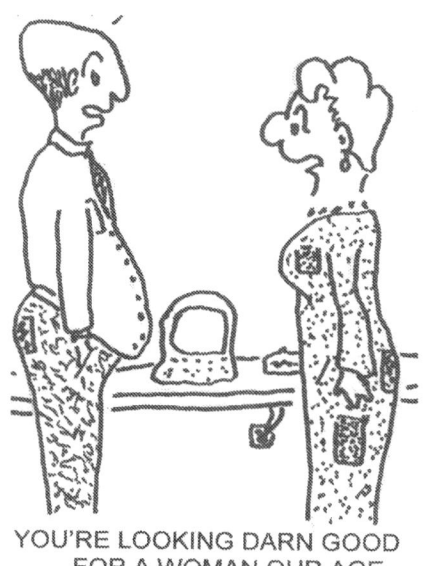

YOU'RE LOOKING DARN GOOD
. . . FOR A WOMAN OUR AGE

[*Sal Seller* doesn't realize his words can wound. Men often see themselves through different eyes than do women.]

DAWN: Small Foundations

Individually established in local communities, to help pay attorney fees, as other foundations provide scholarships. With paid attorneys overseen by a local foundation, better able to afford serving the abused than any who work *pro bono*, <u>the best lawyers in the community</u> will be getting the work. Doing ever better with practice—learning from each other—for the clients who come later. Attorneys making use of tips from those of us who have been there, can help others in similar circumstances learn how to cut off the lawyer who drags things out for the money!

Only the Best

- Those lawyers found best able to help children of indigent mothers, are to be paid at the discretion of DAWN foundation directors living within the community.
- Any are to be encouraged to utilize paralegals and any other staff to cut the billable hours. Streamline the operations.
- When good lawyers can afford to do more of the work they could not do pro bono, somewhat less good lawyers will be inspired to do better work in order to be selected.

As with every other line of work, there are good lawyers as well as bad, and the object is to make the less good, better. (And the already good, the best.)

- Changed laws over time notwithstanding, there still remain too many recent stories of exploitation. By attorneys hired, judges assigned, and courts in general. Supported by people in public office, themselves all too often a part of the abusive situation.

- Other people, other places, document many of those incidents. We will work with them, not duplicating efforts.

Enlightenment

Hope for the future, resides in the gifts made for good causes worldwide and the people handling the distribution.

The <u>Winter 2000 Ford Foundation Report</u> in a special issue on women listed on 27 pages, over 1000 grants made worldwide in just one four month period. With four offices in the Western Hemisphere, five in Africa and six in Asia, no limit was evident in support of every part of the world.

More than 80 grants were female-specific using the word <u>*women*</u>, and another two dozen covered reproductive issues also applying preponderantly to females. Nine targeted violence, mostly of the domestic variety.

A quick count showed some 65 grants made to other foundations—among many more to universities and other educational institutions.

So maybe you want to get into the line with your hand held out?

It doesn't work that way

No more that it did for Sancho Panza carrying a rope in case someone offered him a heifer as he accompanied Don Quijote, it won't now.

Everyone receiving grants had something viable going when starting. They "did their homework" first.

They Were Approached

In the early 1970's the Ford Foundation officers were approached by representatives of the women's movement. The request was made for the same sort of support for women as had been extended to the civil rights movement.

It built from there, with consideration that the needs of women differ from one part of the world to the other. A common theme however, is inequitable treatment, health issues specific to the female, and violence directed at us.

Some countries—too often not ours!—are in advance of others. Especially as a United States Supreme Court decision anchored in the 19th Century denied women what Congress awarded with VAWA.

There is help out there, not only from the Ford Foundation. However, instead of holding our hands out we need to build something first that is worth supporting.

DOMESTIC ABUSE ISN'T ALWAYS
PRIVATE . . . OR PHYSICAL

[<u>*Cory Anders and Cile:*</u> writer/ photographer team. (He tells her and so far has her convinced, that she can't do anything without him.)]

Nonprofit Foundations

Not all **<*.org*>** nonprofits are foundations, though a <u>FOUNDATION</u> is a <u>*NONPROFIT ORGANIZATION*</u> accepting tax deductible contributions, which elected directors disburse to needy recipients. It is done according to bylaws and involves arranging for funding selected applicants.

1. A foundation can be established to help pay attorney fees. As some other foundations provide scholarships.
2. A legal advisor—an attorney—checks the wording of the bylaws herewith available as a free sample outline. This

attorney advises on filing to make the foundation a legal entity.

3. A lawyer may work pro bono. States however, demand a fixed fee for registration, and in Washington State, a filing fee with annual report.

4. A foundation is not monetarily supported by its directors—except by such donations as they may privately and individually care to make.

5. The voting directors of a foundation are elected, unpaid volunteers.

6. As the foundation grows legal advice by single attorney or firm may become necessary on continuing basis, a legitimate expense to the foundation.

7. Ongoing expenses after legal establishment of the foundation include the usual office needs of letterhead, envelopes, postage, etc.—even if all the work is done by volunteers.

8. Though once a foundation attains a certain size—depending upon the funds needed to be handled—a paid Executive Director is selected.

9. A foundation established in a city—San Francisco, Boston, Houston, Miami—may need a hired executive director almost immediately.

10. Not much later, a paid secretary and perhaps treasurer.

11. In small towns or rural communities as ours, all offices filled and duties performed can be done by the elected directors, until that becomes awkward because of size.

12. The bylaws wording for each foundation would change according to venue, but the sample given was Washington-state-legal in the mid-1990s.

13. It can be used as the form from which to work, with each individual foundation needing its own lawyer for overseeing the differences.

Contact of those interested in establishing a local *DAWN—Domestic Abuse Women's Net*—foundation was done by e-mail, with Bcc: to any enthusiastic about the idea not yet out of the domestic violence closet.

All business when possible was done by email or local telephone call. Decisions made most often by consensus rather than vote of the directors, with input by members. Those never subject to abuse, invariably knew some who had been.

A Few Questions

Q: Where would start-up money actually come from? Will it all be local or are we talking grants, etc.?
A: Both local and grants of course, and any other kind of funding that can be devised. "Fund-raisers" of any kind, though for best results these should be handled by another committee.

Q: Who will be eligible for help and will it just be for legal fees?
A: With each foundation independent, decisions will be made locally. But, good directors will understand the most can be helped, by getting the best possible legal help.

Q: What will the requirements be to use this service?

A: The elected foundation directors, once the foundation has gotten funding, will decide just what to support. Not only to get a divorce or separation with decent terms for family members, but to provide the children with protection, by whatever course is taken.

Q: Will area foundations be integrated on the national level— and will each area have to form its own nonprofit?

A: Only an informal connection at the national level in the United States with e-mail contacts is intended for economy sake, with each nonprofit established independently. With a small enough area geographically, local directors can control where the money goes.

Internationally, any information we have available we have tried, not always successfully, to keep updated on the Internet:

http://www.willapadawn.org

Questions are invited. What can be done with our answers, depends on the laws of the various countries.

Q: How soon should an executive board be developed and who chosen?

A: Whenever a number of interested people—preferably mostly women for the necessary insight, perhaps as domestic violence advocates, shelter assistants or triumphant survivors of abuse—can decide on formal bylaws.

Q: Will there be administrative or training conferences?

A: If anyone wants to volunteer to provide them. We have no provisions for holding such at this time. Conferences may be set up later, but they are not in current planning.

Q: What about copyrights?

A: This information has originally been donated for use by the public without restriction, but at individual risk. All presented will not apply equally to everyone. It is the republishing of information and offering it for sale that the copyright is to prevent. Use of the information we provide is encouraged. We believe FREE is a way to get action, as in that way all can afford it.

- Once a local foundation is legally registered, to begin obtaining funding can be done with press releases to local newspapers—and a try for television and radio coverage.
- Press release outlines can be traded, to which local information is to be added. Someone also could try for national radio and television exposure.

I have no legal credentials, nor experience with larger foundations.

Having worked to start a number of small foundations, I was a director for some years of one providing scholarships for higher education to high school students.

Until I made my escape to the domestic violence shelter one July, and subsequent divorce.

Involved with the Veterans of Foreign Wars Voice of Democracy contests through the VFW Auxiliary, I won the local Voice of Democracy contests—essays at the time—while I was a sophomore and senior in high school.

[Parents can injure children's self-esteem . . . as Eleanor Roosevelt knew quite well.]

NONPROFIT FOUNDATION
A domestic violence guide

> *A guide to eliminate domestic violence:*
> 1. What is a Nonprofit Foundation; 2. The Sample Bylaws Outline; 3. Foundation Funding; 4. Grant Access.

DAWN: A net not only for Internet Networking, but a Safety Net spread across the United States. Other countries welcome to adapt as their laws may make possible. The goal is to *protect children everywhere*, by getting them and an abused parent out of an intolerable situation.

One in four marriages in the United States is currently categorized as abusive. Since the problem remains very hidden, that can only be a rough estimate at best.

Statistically, due to historical precedence, women are more often than men, the abused. Ninety-five percent females, in contrast to five percent males.

Not only has the female of our species on average less physical strength, but society has long denied her social equality. Nor accorded her legal recourse.

Women do have more stamina—there has been little alternative so far as survival has concerned. As with other groups discriminated against by society, protective survival traits have developed. And more recently, technology is being used to advantage.

The Internet, with email and browser access to Web sites, has eliminated much of the isolation. At least once escape from an abusive situation has been accomplished.

It is necessary to get action more independent of lawmakers and courts, *in a way the most helpless can afford it*.

Too often lawyers, judges and state agencies supposed to support the abuses, simply victimize them further.

Unscrupulous lawyers for both parties will drag out a separation or divorce for so long as they can, in order to obtain a larger fee. Often to the point of family bankruptcy.

> Such obtain the fee by demand—it has not been earned!

Those with fewer resources are able to attain resolution faster as far as certain lawyers are concerned. And, never having been in the situation before. Even the relatively well-to-do—until they've been to court—do not know to whom to turn.

As our ancestors were wont to say, "There's no use beating a dead horse." Nor billing a bankrupt client.

I DON'T BABYSIT . . . SO TODAY YOU ARE GROWNUP

[Some women, while compassionate, refuse to hide that motherhood and children is not their only ambition in life.]

CONTROL BY BULLIES

Children killing children, all across our nation finally get our attention. The boy in Oregon was 15 and the decision was to try him for murder as an adult. A century ago, many at 15 were adults, with all the rights and responsibilities of self-support and procreation. Boys of 13 became men working 12 hour days, six days a week. Women by the time they were 15 could be married with a child or two of their own, or raising a family of their orphaned siblings.

The Grange at its inception and still, considers young people once they are age 14, mature enough to take full voting membership, and serving as officers.

BLAME THE VICTIM?

But what is a victim? Survivor? A survivor is a victor, certainly. But to survive you need not have been a victim. Hero perhaps for enduring, as a fortunate "hero" has survived.

So often now we read of unfortunates who through health problems or injury live difficult lives and they are called "hero" for doing so.

The difficulty of living with long term abuse is no less than being hampered by a physical or mental disability. Stressful and at least equally depressive.

All too often when the abuse has been violent, with permanent physical injury.

People who have never been in an abusive situation, consider those who have been or are, only as victims. Usually as _stupid_ victims as well. And for those inclined to be controlling, targets for further abuse.

What is not realized is the terrible strength it takes to keep living in the situation when there is no way out. As a prisoner of war, when the signed contract was for love. No way out, except—all too often—being murdered by the abuser.

Or, alternatively, either murder done by, or the suicide of, the abused.

When there are children involved, or elderly parents to protect from the terrible knowledge, the abused will tolerate much for a long and miserable time.

- What is seen as the various fates of dependent children under our current society, allows a good parent little choice but to endure.
- We need to help reform and bend the legal system to support others in the same shoes as we wear. Women who, like us, are always carefully looking out their own windows from behind curtains, and who look over their shoulders whenever fearfully walking down a sidewalk.
- Too many young mothers around our country and world are destitute, unable even to hire a lawyer, while their abusers have control of the entire income and can hire any corrupt attorney to influence judges. Those judges and lawyers often unfeeling, macho womanizers.

The only way to insure justice is to hit the oppressors where it hurts most, in the pocket book. Make it more worthwhile for any who are already as much a help as they can afford. And a spur for improvement of those who are a problem.

The traditional monetary reward can be offered by establishing local foundations nationwide, and eventually worldwide, to collect money for hiring selected attorneys.

- Always the best available, while more learn to improve, even if just for their own enrichment.
  The traditional carrot and stick approach.
- As a beginning before starting the nonprofit, join the accumulating e-mail list of interested parties who want to learn how to set up such foundations in their areas. Let them know you want to be on a Bcc: list.

The concerned working together can bring about in the new millennium, a new DAWN:

Of small Domestic Abuse Women's Nets, simple foundations established in local communities to help pay attorney fees for the needy, as others provide scholarships.

With paid attorneys overseen by a local foundation, better able to afford serving than any who work pro bono, the best lawyers in the community will be getting the work. Doing ever better with practice, for the clients who come later.

1. Tips from those of us who have been there, can help others in similar circumstances learn how to cut off the attorney who drags things out for the money!

2. Those lawyers found best able to help children of indigent mothers, are to be paid at the discretion of DAWN foundation directors living within the community.

3. Once good lawyers can afford to do work they could not do pro bono, somewhat less good lawyers will be inspired to do better work in order to be selected.

4. A far better incentive than they could ever have learned in law school.

5. As with every other line of work, there are good lawyers as well as bad, and the object is to make the less good, better. And the already good, the best.

6. It is those lawyers found best able to help children of indigent mothers, who are to be offered payment to take on certain cases at the discretion of DAWN foundation directors living within the community.

7. Not all those in abusive situations, seeking relief, are indigent. Therefore, an added benefit to the community is the advice the DAWN directorship could dispense—for a fee—to those able to afford asking for it.

8. There is lack of support not only from the criminal justice system, but also from the media, with heads inserted deliberately in the sand.

9. The entire subject of domestic violence—the abuse within families at the root core of violence in the schools and on the streets this current generation—is often written "about" by those not involved in it.

10. Some of us came out of the domestic violence closet partly to protect ourselves.
11. Not that we wanted the notoriety, which we had been avoiding all through an abusive relationship.
12. To make sure instead, that our abuser was caught if anything happened to us.
13. As news stories will tell you happens all too often, despite repeated protection orders and arrests.

> One of the first things learned on entering a domestic violence shelter—either from a crisis support advocate or one of the other abused in residence—is to make some kind of written record of what happened, and keep a detailed record in writing of what occurs in the future.

I had a protection order and was advised by a female state patrol officer to keep it in effect permanently. My written record went, in part, on my Web site—serving as core for establishing DAWN once I found others ready to get involved.

Another function could be to provide guidance for filing a grievance with the State Bar Association, against a lawyer who has not fulfilled his/her contractual duty.

Perhaps a paralegal could be hired to complete necessary forms.

My report to the State Bar Association gave little resolution— but the paperwork provides reason for DAWN not to support one attorney.

YOU'RE JUST LAZY . . .
A "HOUSEWIFE" DOESN'T WORK!

[*Smedley Slye*: has no respect for the work his wife and mother do to keep the large family operating smoothly. Some people consider the monetary contribution they make to the family is all that counts.]

Sample

BYLAWS OF Centerville DAWN
HOMETOWN COUNTY, STATE OF WHEREVER

ARTICLE I
Name and Duration

SECTION 1. The Name of this organization shall be Centerville DAWN: Domestic Abuse Women's net, and its duration shall be perpetual.

ARTICLE II
Purpose and Mission

SECTION 1. The purpose of this Corporation shall be to receive and encourage gifts, endowments and bequests for implementing funding and utilization for grants to lawyers, in support of protecting children in custody cases.

ARTICLE III
Membership

SECTION 1. Membership in this Corporation shall be open to individuals in the community in sympathy with its purposes, accepted for a mailing list.

ARTICLE IV
Officers and Directors

SECTION 1. The business and property of Centerville DAWN: Domestic Abuse Women's net, shall be managed by a board of not less than five and not more than nine Directors -- an uneven number -- elected at the annual meeting by simple majority vote of the membership of the Corporation in attendance.

SECTION 2. All Officers and Directors shall be members of the organization.

The term of Officers shall be one year.

The term of Directors shall be three years after the first three years.

- The first elected Directors shall have 1, 2 and 3 year terms.
- There shall be one or two -- one year terms, two or three -- two year terms, and two to four -- three year terms.

SECTION 3. The Directors shall elect Officers from their group at the first meeting following the annual meeting in November.

- They shall assume their respective offices at the January meeting and serve a one year term.
- They shall be a President, Vice President, Secretary and Treasurer, or a combination of the last two as Secretary/Treasurer.

- They shall have the usual duties, authority and responsibility normally exercised by such Officers of a Nonprofit Corporation.

SECTION 4. The board of Directors of the Corporation shall hold monthly board meetings, and such special meetings as the board shall deem necessary for the competent management of the affairs of the Corporation.

SECTION 5. Each member of the Board of Directors shall possess one vote in matters coming before the Board.
Notice in writing of the proposed removal of a Director must be given to such Director two weeks [14 days] prior to the date of the meeting at which such removal is to be voted on.

> Such notice to the Director must state
> cause for the proposed removal.

SECTION 6. The unexcused absence from three consecutive meetings of the Board of Directors shall be due cause for removal of a Director.

SECTION 7. Any vacancy occurring on the Board of Directors by reason of death, resignation or removal of a Director or Officer/ Director shall be filled by the remaining Board members.

> Such appointee shall serve during the unexpired term
> of the Director whose position has become vacant.

ARTICLE V
Meetings

SECTION 1. All monthly meetings shall be open to the public with only the Board of Directors voting.

SECTION 2. Voting on amendments done at regular monthly meetings however, shall be by the entire membership present.

SECTION 3. The annual meeting shall be held immediately after the November monthly meeting, by the Members of the Corporation.

> Members shall be notified in writing at least two weeks prior to the date of the meeting.

SECTION 4. A special meeting of the Corporation may be called by the Board of Directors and all members must be given at least two weeks notice.

SECTION 5. At any regular monthly meeting of the directors of the Corporation, those present shall constitute a quorum for the transaction of business.

SECTION 6. An annual meeting quorum shall consist of non-board members exceeding the number of Board members present.

SECTION 7. ROBERT'S RULES OF ORDER REVISED, when not in conflict with these bylaws, shall govern the proceedings of this Corporation.

ARTICLE VI
Programs and Fiscal Management

SECTION 1. The fiscal year of the Foundation shall be January 1 through December 31.

SECTION 2. The program policies and procedures approved by the Board which govern general and specific business operations shall be placed in a manual independent of the Bylaws, maintained as current standard operating procedures.

SECTION 3. An Executive Director shall be chosen by the Board to serve as chief operating officer of the Foundation and chief staff officer of the Board and of all Board Committees. The Executive Director may serve as liaison between the Board and agencies. With the approval of the Board, the Executive Director shall designate a staff member to assume duties and responsibilities of the Executive Director in the latter's absence.

SECTION 4. At the discretion of the Board, any or all officers, agents or employees may be required to give bond for the faithful performance of his/her/their fiduciary duties in such amount as with such sureties as the Board may prescribe.

SECTION 5. The Executive Director shall prepare periodic reports of all receipts, disbursements, transactions and end of period balances to the membership. At the annual meeting the President of the Foundation shall make an annual report of all business conducted by the Foundation.

SECTION 6. Upon notification of receipt of new assets or of the desire for the transfer of existing assets, the Executive Director shall proceed in accordance with policy and procedures of the Board.

SECTION 7. The receipt, holding, transfer, accounting and custodianship of securities shall be in accordance with the provision of these Bylaws and with policies and procedures recommended by the Board.

> This Corporation may employ and retain proper advisors to counsel with, advise and aid the Board in the proper receipt, holding, transferring, accounting and maintenance of securities of this Corporation.

SECTION 8. The Executive Director shall disburse funds or resources governed by the Bylaws only upon due authorization of vouchers, or written directives, or recommendations by the Board. Authorizations shall be required for checks, securities and other financial instruments as well as deeds, trust agreements, contracts, leases, licenses and other financial devices.

SECTION 9. The Executive Director shall maintain a complete and current inventory of all fiscal, financial and physical assets.

SECTION 10. There shall be at least an annual audit by an independent auditor, of all books, records and transaction documents as directed by the Board. All such records shall be available for inspection by any voting members through the Executive Director, upon request.

ARTICLE VII
Gift Policy

SECTION 1. All gifts shall be accepted by the Executive Director subject to the approval of the Board. Such transfers of assets not considered ordinary shall be deferred until advance approval of the Board is obtained.

SECTION 2. All gifts which require the payment of annuity amount or other charge from the funds or resources of the Foundation shall be made only from the income and/or principal of the transferred asset itself.

SECTION 3. The Foundation will not provide appraisals to donors for non-cash gifts. Appraisal is authorized only for Foundation accounting purposes.

ARTICLE VIII
Dissolution

SECTION 1. In event of voluntary dissolution, the net assets will be disbursed as follows: To one or more charitable organizations serving disadvantaged children in the specified area.

ARTICLE IX
Amendments

SECTION 1. Amendments to these bylaws may be made at any meeting of the general membership by a majority vote of those present, after notification in writing to each member at least two weeks before the meeting at which the voting is to take place.

PROHIBITION IN SHARING
IN CORPORATION EARNINGS

No Member, Director, Officer or Employee of the Corporation, or any other private individual shall receive at any time any of the net earnings or pecuniary profit from operation of the Corporation, provided, that this shall not prevent the payment to any such person of such reasonable compensation or services rendered to or for the Corporation in effecting any of its purposes as shall be fixed by the Board of Directors; and no such person or person shall be entitled to share in the distribution of any of the Corporation assets upon dissolution of the Corporation.

All members of the Corporation shall be deemed to have expressly consented and agreed that upon such dissolution or winding up of the affairs of the Corporation, whether voluntary or involuntary, the assets of the Corporation, after all debts have been satisfied, then remaining in the hands of the

Board of Directors shall be distributed, transferred, conveyed, delivered and paid over, in such amounts as the Board of Directors may determine or as may be determined by a Court of competent jurisdiction upon application of the Board of Directors, exclusively to organizations which would then qualify under the provisions of Section 501 (c) (3) of the Internal Revenue Code and its regulations as they now exist or as they may hereafter amended.

(Exempt activities.) Notwithstanding any other provision of these Bylaws, no Member, Director, Officer, Employee or Representative of this Corporation shall take any action or carry on any activity by or on behalf of the Corporation not permitted to be taken or carried on by any organization exempt under Section 501 (c) (2) of such Code and Regulations as they now exist or may hereafter be amended.

Adopted at the [day]_____[month]_____[year]_____meeting of Centerville Chapter DAWN: Domestic Abuse Women's Net.

_____
President

_____
Vice President

_____
Secretary

_____
Treasurer

The above is not the bylaws of Willapa Chapter DAWN, but only an approximation of how they might be written.

WANT TO HOLD YOUR BABY? NO.
BUT I WILL IN AN EMERGENCY

[*Nerda*, little *Nerdy* and baby *Nerdella*. (She doesn't have it all together, but she loves children dearly and thinks everyone else does too.]

> [Matthew 13.12] Who has, to him is given
> and from the have nots, is taken away.

- If the times haven't changed that much, we can work to make them change.

> It can't be said too often:

> # "No one deserves to be abused!"

> # OPPORTUNITY

An opportunity we were told about arose soon after our beginning, which wasn't in Willapa DAWN's originally stated purpose. It was too good not to take advantage.

Still without funds beyond the fees needed for recognition, monetary support became available with a deadline, to assist small home-based or storefront businesses get started or expand.

When that didn't work out after all, the advisor who had told us, stepped in to provide help. A businessman who could provide computer upgrades with additional software, an Internet connection for a period of time, or a PC if there was none. With our nonprofit status from the IRS, we could accept used equipment for him to refurbish.

<u>How could we refuse to take advantage?</u> A single parent too often needs to make a living in some way, since even if the courts supply support it all too often may not be there.

Help any small business, and it can take the stress off a good marriage. Or prepare for one that terminates—by the death or disability of a relationship partner.

The people we found to help were not in abusive situations. All to the good, as those we found later who were, would be lost—unidentified—in the mix.

Website listings

Any business, accepting assistance or not, which agreed to be listed http://www.willapadawn.org/bizlinks.htm with a link on our pages, was added.

Each used the same form giving information for contact. Not only their mailing, emailing and website link listings, but owner and directions when necessary. Each business did not necessarily have all those, so we used just what each one had

An important listing was the business of one of our first directors, The BOOK Store, where the first copies of this self-published copyright book **NONPROFIT ORGANIZATION, Setting Up a Charitable Foundation** were offered for sale.

The BOOK Store

http://www.willapadawn.org/bookstore
Betty Miller
Owner

1013 W Robert Bush Drive
General Delivery
(The river side of Highway 101)
South Bend WA 98586

Telephone 1.360.875.6675
E-mail: bookstore@reachone.com

Commentary

1. In the beginning a DAWN foundation group will not need an Executive Director—this is usually a full time paid position—and some of the smaller ones never will require one.

2. The smallest Foundation will need only three directors and the largest should be able to make do with no more than fifteen.

3. Always an uneven number, for voting purposes. So there will not be a tie.

4. Use the above model only as a rough, customizing as needs warrant.

5. Have the Foundation Bylaws as you have prepared them, checked by an attorney after the elected Directors have voted approval, and before they are finally accepted.

6. A recently retired lawyer may be willing to do the necessary advising without charge. Or, someone who just recently passed the bar examination may find association with the foundation a better career move than accepting a fee. (You can always point out the donation is tax exempt.) Negotiate *everything*. Money saved helps the foundation.

7. A relatively small amount of money as Initial Funding is needed to establish a foundation with the Internal Revenue Service.

INITIAL FUNDING

After establishing a Nonprofit Foundation by use of a Sample Bylaws Outline, the amount to cover the fee necessary for the Internal Revenue Service should be deposited at a local banking establishment, along with the minimum to continue keeping the account open once that fee is withdrawn.

I believe the amount was $150.00 a few years ago in my state. Perhaps now $350.00. It would of course vary from one state to another.

Collect this money anywhere you can, in 1, 5, 10, 25 dollar increments. Do fund raising events like car washes, rummage and bake sales. Request help from ministers of local churches. See if a supermarket will let you set up a table near the entrance. Ask businesses to provide space for your labeled donation jars.

Ask the newly elected directors, if you can't get enough from the public. Though publicity should more than take care of it quite soon. There are many who were or are being abused and not "out of the closet" who will be pleased to contribute, even if anonymously. Or friends and family members who they want to help out of an intolerable situation.

Check with all banks and credit unions within the community, asking for the best deal they can make you for a growing nonprofit organization. You want to check interest rates, and penalties. After comparisons, sign the term contract with the one the Foundation Directors choose as best.

> # Name the account, "[*Hometown*] *DAWN*."

You will use it a long time, not only for setup.

M' WIFE'S NO HOUSEKEEPER

[*Meander* is charming—and a pretty nice guy when he is sober—but is lazy and content to let Tukwila carry all the load of their relationship.]

FOUNDATION FUNDING

Funding is not the problem it might at first seem, because there are many individuals and corporations who need the tax deduction that making donations to nonprofit organizations can provide.

GRANTS:

Accrual is not immediate. It takes time to research where to apply, to write effective grant applications, and for decisions of the grant funding foundations among all the applications received that year.

Foundations fund each other. For example, in my very small city the Raymond Foundation established by the founding family, distributes moneys annually.

The Weyerhaeuser sawmill long on the downtown waterfront and a parent foundation distributes grants also. Elsewhere too, since the corporation is so widespread.

A DAWN foundation would be set up to fund individual concerns, and not to include funding another foundation.

Sometimes matching funds are required for grants. These can be provided with volunteer work, rather than in cash. Keep track of everyone's time spent on DAWN and you will find places where it will count.

In June 1999 we learned my county received a grant of nearly $30,000 to fight substance abuse and violence.

The grant provided by Washington State Community, Trade and Economic Development, was received by Pacific County Public Health and Human Services. With stipulation made of at least a local 25% matching obligation. There were over 9,175 volunteers involved across my state during the year—and DAWN foundations should have had no problem in qualifying.

BEQUESTS:

They may take much longer before any begin coming in, since Wills are made while the prospective donor is still in sound health of mind and body.

ORGANIZATIONAL DONATIONS:

- Go to any auxiliary, church or fraternal order to which you belong, as an insider.
- Recruit interested insider friends to take you as a guest, to present your plea to other organizations.
- Older groups are good to contact, not so much for possible bequests as networking, because on average women—usually more interested in family protection issues—outlive men.
- Women whether retired from paid employment or never having worked outside the home, are much less apt to stop working entirely. They can quite often be persuaded to volunteer.

Older groups are good to contact, not so much for possible bequests as the opportunity for networking.

These groups are more likely to be proportionately greater female, because on average women—usually more interested in family protection issues as well as more apt to be among the abused—outlive men.

As well, they may have daughters or granddaughters in abusive relationships.

Some women will be divorced, and a percentage of widows will be sympathetic because they outlived their abuser husbands without the world ever knowing the miserable married life they led. They may even be well-to-do.

Advise everyone of the name of the account and its location—that anonymous donations will also be appreciated.

```
ALWAYS TELL EVERYONE
WHERE DONATIONS CAN BE SENT
```

```
CORPORATIONS:
```

Including companies such as <u>Weyerhaeuser</u>—with tree farms all over my county and in the much of the rest of our country. <u>Boeing</u> with locations in Seattle, Everett and Auburn, as well as in other states. Shipyards—and yes, Internet moguls such as are located in Redmond, Washington. Any who make so much money they have to give it away.

From the Silicon Valley, Silicon Forest—and more—they give money away for tax saving purposes . . . and with much publicity.

NO ONE DESERVES ABUSE

[*Nerda* and people like her after long hiding the abuse, and finally confiding in friends, may find them completely surprised and often disbelieving.]

Corporations will actually seek you out. Tell you about where to try for grants and sometimes make outright donations. (It is tax deductible, remember?) You are doing them a favor by asking.

Tax deductible money given away was earned as profits, from the things or services we and their other customers bought.

Gates and Allen of Microsoft are not technically giving way their own ethically earned money, but the extra cash you and I paid because we needed their software as a virtual monopoly, to access the internet and for other business purposes.

Years ago I worked as a Service Representative in Seattle for the telephone company and we received instructions on all facets of dealing with customers. Except one.

"If someone calls the company a monopoly, you are on your own . . . because they are right."

- Some businesses are monopolies and you deal with them accordingly. Then there are the others; they have competition.
- It takes a different strategy to obtain help from competing organizations of any kind.
- Publicity and sponsorship can be of great benefit to anyone.
- It is up to you to point that out convincingly.

HOW TO START

Always dress conservatively in a businesslike manner. Dress as though you are applying for an executive position with the company.

Remember, you are successful in your own field and a consultant donating your time to this worthy cause.

You want to look mature. Gray hair and wrinkles are not an obstacle. Neither is being retired from your original field of expertise.

People need to know that you are working not for yourself, but for others. Which—as a director, you are—providing a valuable service for the organization and community.

Don't worry about nervousness. It won't be noticed as much as you think, and those who do will either be sympathetic because they've been in the same position, or awed at your bravery because they have not.

It gets easier with practice. And if you stumble, what will they do, beat you black and blue? You've been through worse.

Take heart from the fact that those you want to help, are still in the midst of misery.

Form a speakers' bureau of all the directors. Book the more timid to the easy appointments at first—until with practice some of you are ready for Oprah and Geraldo.

Make appointments with publishers, managing editors, or as high on the publishing food chain as you can get.

WORKING WITH ANGER

An observation found in a book: <u>"Depression is Anger turned inward."</u>

Controlling anger can make it work for us, rather than our becoming depressed.

It is a position from which to recruit others in our same situation. Comparing our reasons for anger, we can determine to take action in eliminating the problem.

The action of control turns anger upside down and inside out. Gives us joy, equal to replaced anger.

It doesn't necessarily take a lawyer to prepare to begin a nonprofit organization. Nor a paralegal. (I am neither.)

The first thing to do is locate a number of local people—two or three as minimum. Next, approach some sympathetic acquaintances to get involved as members from which a board can be selected by vote. Not only those who have suffered domestic violence, but talk about it to ministers of various churches in the community, fraternal organizations, attorneys, grandparents who want the best for everyone's kids.

Only if you can't get the needed expertise from recruited members to do the filing with the state, IRS and all to make things legal, will it be necessary to find an outside lawyer.

DONATIONS OTHER THAN MONEY:

Accept only those donations for which you are given permission to sell, that don't tie up storage space. Pieced quilts and other craft items can be raffled.

Have along a simple Press Release with the most salient points, and ask for someone to interview you.

ALWAYS TAKE ALONG YOUR BUSINESS CARDS

Be very careful of those who want to impose conditions on the donation. You are probably safer in just turning them down.

- **Real estate** can cost more to service than it is worth as income.
- **Stock**—listed on Wall Street and not cattle or grocery items which can be sold to the highest bidder or at market price—fluctuates.
- You don't want to gamble with helpless children's lives.

RESOURCES:

According to a press release from **GrantSmart** dated March 28, 2000 from San Diego, CA, as of March 13, 2000, federal legislation requires private foundations to make their IRS Form 990-PFs available to the public.

President John Downing of California-based Canyon Research, operating on a nonprofit basis and in collaboration with the Internal Revenue Service, posted private foundation tax returns, IRS Form 990-PFs, on the Internet.

"A review of these returns reveals that assets held by all private foundations was over $290 billion in 1998. Normally, a foundation issues 5% of its assets in grants. This corresponds to nearly $15 billion available in grants in 1998 alone."

A tool for researching private foundation returns, the website (new at the time) had data on private foundation activities of interest to grantseekers, philanthropic organizations, and individual donors.

The Internet continues to grow in usefulness, as we search periodically.

Members of private foundations who registered can log-in and verify information provided in the Database correct for their organization. Correct inaccuracies in the existing data and provide supporting information about their organization.

This information is then added to the Database, giving even the smallest private foundation a presence on the Internet.

Web Address: http://www.grantsmart.org
E-Mail: info@grantsmart.org

1. Check with the state Attorney General for information and state forms.
2. Find Form 1023 to file for 501(c)(3) status with the IRS at http://www.irs.gov and for more information go to http://www.irs.gov/prod/forms_pubs/pubs/p5570307.htm

PERSISTANCE

The Internal Revenue Service won't make this easy for you. They will be glad to take your fee, even a second time—non-refundable if you made a mistake—but want to certify as few 501(c)3 nonprofit organizations as possible and will make things very difficult.

This is when an attorney is worth the fee to the organization itself!

There is lack of support not only from governmental agencies and the criminal justice system, but also recognition by the media.

MEDIA COVERAGE

- **Letters to the editor may be ignored or at best accepted free, condensed and rewritten.**
- **<u>Newspapers will not pay local writers to set the record straight in presenting viewpoints concerning the victims.</u>**
- **<u>Nor from the survivors of Domestic Violence.</u>**

Yes, many survivors of abuse are still frightened and in hiding.

But, some others of us across the country and world who can write from personal experience, have come out of the domestic violence closet, having faced that all we have to left to lose is our lives. Which were at risk before our escapes.

Instead, some newspapers print syndicated writers attacking those in recovery from domestic abuse. It makes "good copy" to blame the oppressed.

It costs less to buy syndicated copy and there is no writer or cartoonist to deal with personally as happens when local material is bought.

Syndicates on average gets 50%, the producer of the feature, the other half. (Some syndicates and certain feature providers may have a slightly different arrangement.)

You can complain to a syndicate or newspaper, by USPS, email, FAX or telephone. Use the 800 number if they have one. Usually they have to pay for your call, but that doesn't mean they will pay attention to your viewpoint.

HIT THEM IN THE POCKETBOOK!
Holding the Purse-strings Gives Control

Most of us now live in a one-newspaper-community where we are captive to a single newspaper that will be delivered to us. We can't even go to the competition! Dropping a subscription may not do much good since while newspaper readership keeps dropping advertising rates are being regularly raised to make up for it.

Advertisers pay for their ads with money they earned locally, from you.

Instead, contact those who put ads in your local newspaper. (Biggest ones and/or the ones for whom you are customer, first.) Email if they have a published username, with a Cc: to the newspaper. The syndicate too.

POSTER CHILD

It is common for an individual or organization to choose a cause to promote.

We tripped over, fell into ours

The first two years, Willapa DAWN joined Willapa Grange # 527 in celebrating one day of the Eleanor Roosevelt Day weekend. In 2005, due to the loss—by poor health and death—of a number of the local Grange officers, DAWN moved the celebration to a local restaurant.

In June 1994 the Washington State Grange at the annual convention passed resolution 94-62—one of 21 adopted—to honor Anna Eleanor Roosevelt on the Second Monday of each August. In November the National Grange adopted the resolution, and posted it on their Web site.

OBVIOUS CONNECTION

For the Domestic Abuse Women's Net the connection between Anna Eleanor Roosevelt and DAWN was obvious.

For all her family background of wealth, prominence and good works, Eleanor Roosevelt had lived an abused life nearly from birth, and her marriage only compounded the problems.

Eleanor's:

1. Mother sneered and laughed at the serious child, before dying young and leaving her and her brother to the care of a cold grandmother.
2. Father, was an alcoholic who died when she was ten.
3. Mother-in-law imposed her will on Eleanor and the grandchildren.
4. Husband cheated on her, lied that he had reformed to get a commitment and continued the cheating.
5. Daughter hid her father's infidelity from her mother.

THE PUBLIC LOVED HER

Including Harry S Truman, the president of the United States who succeeded her husband. And eventually, those in the entire world she served.

> Not a victim—Eleanor Roosevelt was a
> SURVIVOR as are all those successfully
> escaping domestic abuse

The W.A.S.H. Rag

The <u>Women Against Sexual Harassment</u> newsletter has given out "Anita Awards" (named after Anita Hill) and any DAWN group could stage an annual—or quarterly—ceremony to present an impressive certificate and bouquet of flowers to a good judge, lawyer or person in Congress.

And yes, it is also acceptable to give flowers to a man.

Advising the media ahead of time of course, but also with our own photographer at hand to prepare news releases—if the media doesn't show.

It can't be said too often:
"No one deserves to be abused!"

ARGUMENTS

Personal Bill of Rights

- The right to be treated with respect
- The right not to take responsibility for anyone else's problems or bad behavior
- The right to get angry
- The right to say "No"
- The right to make mistakes
- The right to have feelings, opinions and convictions

- The right to change mind or decide on different course of action
- The right to negotiate for change
- The right to ask for emotional support or help
- The right to protest unfair treatment or criticism

Some statistical reasons to give when promoting a local DAWN foundation, to be made up mostly of women but also serving a minority of deserving males.

Math Problem

1. Five percent of men in the United States are abused in their familial relationships.
2. One of every four men is an abuser of a woman with whom he has a relationship.
3. Disregarding factors as violence on television and access to guns, X number of teenagers have been raised in abusive homes.
4. Of every 100 in your child or grandchild's school, Y will become productive adults anyway.
5. Find Z

Z is the number of young people who will:
- A: choose suicide
- B: attempt murder
- C: both.

Home school the children? Ah, but they will go to McDonalds, to the post office, to the state park. They _will_ meet adults who grew up in abusive homes.

Published Internet Statistics, May 1999

- Fathers of babies born to teens are significantly older than the mothers.
- Adult males create a large portion of unplanned teen pregnancies. No one is being held responsible. Taxpayers pay support.

The figures can seem contradictory.

1. Of all those younger than 20 who give birth, about two-thirds are 18 and 19 years old, and eighty percent have a partner whose age is within five years of their own.
2. Twenty percent of 18 and 19 year olds give birth to children of fathers more than five years older.
3. A much wider age gap occurs with the youngest mothers:

- For mothers age 15-19, the fathers are an average of 3.7 years older.
- For mothers age 13-14, the fathers are an average of 4.6 years older.
- For mothers age 11-12, the fathers are an average of 9.8 years older.

Married to her or not, the older man is more likely to be controlling and abusive. The young mother is less able to cope. Immaturity at any age, male and female alike can often be traced back to an abusive childhood home. When no one is being held responsible, the taxpayers pay the price.

After beginning Willapa Chapter DAWN, Domestic Abuse Women's Net and registering with the state, it evolved naturally to include as illustrious example the best known female survivor of all, Eleanor Roosevelt. In her lifetime, First Lady of the World but still little appreciated in her own country.

Originally, honoring Eleanor Roosevelt with a day on the national calendar was an idea that came to me in the late 1970s, an overseas member of the National Press Club in Washington DC, having a column published in a daily newspaper—but in a foreign country.

Hardly the place to get support across the United States, so I waited until repatriation in October 1984 and longer, until once more I had a newspaper column being published. Over time, I was being published in three different newspapers.

Though first I started my own small publishing business in order to establish a reputation. It was still far to early for Print-On-Demand, and the World wide Web was restricted to the government and scholars.

Books by Anne Print-On-Demand
http://www.authorhouse.com BOOK STORE
http://www.authorhouse.co.uk BOOK SHOP
Or borrow the books from your library

Autographed copies may be ordered from
bookstore@reachone.com

AuthorHouse books are available from Amazon.com, in libraries, and from major booksellers across the United States.
Internationally, through Ingram.

Intimate Reflections
Two years at the Panama Canal

The last big hiring of canal personnel after one of the earlier periodic slowdowns, with families arrived the summer of 1967 from everywhere across the United States. Their story from 1967 to 1969 includes the Panama Revolution of 1968.

While many throughout the county that rainy season were ill with the pandemic Hong Kong flu the Panamanian military staged a coup. Days after the third inauguration of the three times elected president, Arnulfo Arias, he was once again ousted and Panama had a military government.

That revolution was inexorably followed by elimination of the Canal Zone and the gradual withdrawal of the United States for complete Panamanian sovereignty in 2000.

ISBN 1-4208-9268-1 (Paperback)

Something Fishy
At the Panama Canal

A decades long adventure during which only those who lived it know for sure where history ends and fiction begins—and they don't tell. Canal operation statistics are accurate, the real names are historical and you will recognize them. Though fictitious names are used not to protect the innocent, but rather, some who may not be.

(What is it that lives in the canal, where did it come from, and why are all those ships waiting beyond the normal anchorage anyway? How dared someone use that in the official **Panama Canal Review***—and how does the author get away with using it?)*

ISBN 1-4259-2714-9 (Paperback)

TERRALIMBO
Out of Time

A science fiction/time-travel adventure fantasy—worldwide and beyond—rollicking romp through past, present, and future with a catastrophic detailing of what had been one canal pilot's worst nightmare, with technological possibilities presentation of radio and computer manipulations. No physical restrictions, discomforts, disabilities, infirmities. Emotions and remembered hungers remain; erotic drive is only a memory, even the terrors inflicted are rooted in innocence. (*The discussion by fictitious characters covering the historic 1959 failed Galapagos Island colonization attempt as reported in Pacific Northwest newspapers— giving follow-up information the newspapers have never published.*)

ISBN 1-4259-2042-X (Paperback)

Fletter Cove
Romance & Relationships

Love stories dear and sweet, and other relationship tales of abuse, the coping with insurmountable odds and the triumph of survivors –of any age, as couples and groups, through the ages, world- and galaxy- and universe-wide. Sometimes with surprise of happy endings for all, even the seemingly undeserving. Short stories and verse, with love prevailing.

Bath and barnyard situations where pre-teens and the very old can share snickers to the disgust of those between. Paradox. Even a "Once upon a time" fairytale.

There is something—without using the usual four-letter-words—to offend nearly everyone.

ISBN 1-4259-6214-9 (Paperback)

Intimate Reflections
Tales Told Out of School

A highly personal account of living through the Great Depression and World War II with parents a loving couple in a happy marriage in precarious health who knew their risk of not living to raise a family—mother an *enemy alien* distrusted by neighbors and AEF-Asia veteran father who had served in Siberia planning escape into the hills in event of invasion—when the landmark county courthouse since restored and on the historic register, with its unique "tiffany glass" interior dome, quickly camouflaged while the FBI came to the coastal community, checking on sabotage.

ISBN 978-1-4259-7265-3 (Paperback)

Member NSNC, National Association of Newspaper
Columnists

www.ingramcontent.com/pod-product-compliance
Lightning Source LLC
Chambersburg PA
CBHW021902170526
45157CB00005B/1923